THE BANTAM LIBRARY
of Culinary Arts

SPICES
seeds & barks

JILL NORMAN

BANTAM BOOKS

TORONTO • NEW YORK • LONDON • SYDNEY • AUCKLAND

SPICES: SEEDS & BARKS

A BANTAM BOOK/PUBLISHED BY ARRANGEMENT WITH
DORLING KINDERSLEY LIMITED

PRINTING HISTORY
DORLING KINDERSLEY EDITION
PUBLISHED IN GREAT BRITAIN IN 1989

BANTAM EDITION/MAY 1990

EDITOR GWEN EDMONDS
DESIGNER MATTHEWSON BULL
PHOTOGRAPHER DAVE KING

ART DIRECTOR STUART JACKMAN

LIBRARY OF CONGRESS CATALOGING-IN-PUBLICATION DATA

NORMAN, JILL.
SPICES: SEEDS & BARKS
THEIR USE IN FLAVORING TRADITIONAL AND EXOTIC DISHES /
JILL NORMAN.
P. CM. — (THE BANTAM LIBRARY OF CULINARY ARTS)
"DORLING KINDERSLEY EDITION PUBLISHED IN GREAT BRITAIN 1989" — T.P. VERSO
INCLUDES INDEX.
ISBN 0—553—05738—3
1. SPICES. 2. COOKERY, INTERNATIONAL.
I. TITLE. II. TITLE
SPICES — SEEDS AND BARKS. III. SERIES.
TX406.N686 1990
641.6'383—DC20
89—6809   CIP

PRINTED AND BOUND IN HONG KONG
0 9 8 7 6 5 4 3 2 1

CONTENTS

INTRODUCTION

THE PROFUSION OF SPICES *in any Far Eastern bazaar or North African souk is overwhelming. Westerners are used to buying spices in small jars and packets, but in Asia and Africa they are displayed by the sackful in small specialty stalls or shops. Quality may vary, but usually high-grade and unadulterated spices are available, and sampling the products is encouraged. It is almost always whole spices that are sold, for people still grind and blend spices at home for their daily requirements.*

Freshly ground spices are much more aromatic than powders that have been kept for some time; once ground, spices quickly lose their volatile oils and also their flavor.

Spice mixtures vary according to the region and the dish. Undoubtedly India has the greatest number of masalas, or spice blends, which give the local foods their character. A masala may consist of whole spices, as might be used to flavor a pilaf, or ground, as in Madras curry powder or Punjabi garam masala or panch phoron from Bengal. Neighboring Afghanistan uses chat masala, a blend derived from garam masala, while Hindus who migrated to the West Indies have developed more elaborate versions incorporating local ingredients. The spices used in Indian blends are roasted first; this makes them easier to grind, improves the aroma and also makes them easier to digest.

China has a five-spice powder, a blend of fennel, star anise, cassia, Sichuan pepper and cloves, which is used in many fish and meat dishes. The Japanese use shichimi to flavor their noodles and soups—a mixture of red pepper, sansho pods, dried tangerine peel, poppy seeds, sesame seeds and dried nori seaweed.

Until the last century many European households had their jars of "kitchen pepper," a blend of ginger, pepper, cloves, nutmeg, cinnamon and allspice, which was mixed with salt when required. Spice mixes also found their way into pickles and preserves. Recipes for pickled mushrooms, walnuts, barberries, onions, cabbage, radish pods abound in 18th-century books. Indian pickles and chutneys, ketchups from Southeast Asia, brought back by East India merchants, gained popularity, and imitations were tried at home. Eliza Smith's melon mangoes were spiced with garlic, mustard, pepper and allspice (The Compleat Housewife, 1727); Hannah Glasse's curry of rabbit or chicken, with pepper and dry-roasted coriander (The Art of Cooking Made Plain and Easy 1747). Miss Smith's English Katchup was an approximation of the oriental original, using anchovies, shallots, spices, vinegar and white wine. Sometimes the liquid in which vegetables were pickled was used as a piquant seasoning,

English mustard label
c. 1900

and eventually the liquid came to be bottled as a kind of ketchup to be added to sauces instead of adding spices to the dish while it cooked. These were the forerunners of the store sauces so popular in the 19th century. Bottle sauces were soon prepared commercially; Harvey's sauce and Lazenby's anchovy essence were among the first, followed by Worcestershire sauce and later by Tabasco.

ANISE

*A*NISE (Pimpinella anisum) *is thought to be native to the Levant but has long been cultivated in North Africa and Europe and was introduced into North America where the Shakers grew it as a medicinal crop. It was the traditional cake spice of ancient Rome. Although known in the East, it is not much used. Star anise provides the same flavor; in India anise itself is just called "foreign fennel."*

The very small anise seeds may have a surprisingly "explosive" taste when chewed whole as a digestive, but that taste, sweet and spicy in equal measure, has long been a great favorite with children, in cakes, breads and sweets, even cough medicines. Adult preference goes to the liqueurs, which are claimed as the national drink by most Mediterranean countries.

Anise

CARAWAY

*C*ARAWAY (Carum carvi) *has grown wild in Europe and Asia from the far north to Iran and the Himalayas and was used in the Stone Age at least 5,000 years ago. Holland is the main exporter now; the major consumers are Germany and Austria, but it was popular in Elizabethan England: in Henry IV:2 "a dish of caraways" is offered with an apple.*

Like many other aromatic seeds, caraway is a member of the umbellifer family. Its narrow ridged seed has a warm and rather sweet but also sharp taste, which livens up dumplings or cabbage and makes a pleasant contrast in such diverse foods as rye bread, stewed apples, cheese and cookies. It counteracts the fat of pork or goose, and coated with sugar is chewed as a digestive or breath freshener. The Far East uses cumin rather than caraway.

Caraway

CARDAMOM &

*C*ARDAMOM (Elettaria cardamomum) *is a member of the ginger family, native of the evergreen rain forests of southern India and Sri Lanka. The only other exporting country is Guatemala. It is harvested every few weeks, before the next batch of seeds is fully ripe, and the drying process is a slow and laborious one, which prevents the capsules from splitting. This makes cardamom the most expensive spice after saffron and vanilla. Brown cardamoms from several related species are grown in southern China and Southeast Asia. Their flavor is inferior to that of true cardamom.*

The dark and sticky seeds retain their warmly aromatic but spicy essence best in the green husk. The paler the husk, the older the seed.
Commercial ground cardamom is made of both husk and seed, and best avoided.

Cardamom

Main users of cardamom are the Swedes (for baking), the Arabs (who pour their coffee over it) and the Indians who use it in sweets, pilafs and curries. Cardamom is a remarkably versatile spice.

GRAINS OF PARADISE

*G*RAINS OF PARADISE (Amomum
meleġueta) *is the only true
spice in this book to hail from Africa.
The plant grows around the Gulf
of Guinea, on the Melegueta , or
Pepper, Coast. Ghana remains
the main producer. The rather
fibrous fruit contains a sour
pulp full of brown seeds with
small white tips. These
seeds are the spice.*

Grains of paradise

Although known in overland
trade in the 13th century, it was
rare until Portuguese traders
brought it to Europe in 1460 as
a pepper substitute
that caught
on fast.

Brown cardamom

The pungently peppery
nature of the grains was much
appreciated in spiced wine, with
ginger and cinnamon. It was
misused to give false strength to
malt liquors.

CELERY SEED

*C*ELERY (Apium graveolens) *grows wild through all of central and southern Europe, Asia, Africa and South America. It was not until the 16th century that the Italians managed to breed the bitterness out of the wild variety and cultivation began, and only in the 19th century did celery become generally used in England and the United States.*

Celery

Most celery is harvested in its first year, as a vegetable and herb, but only in the second year does it develop a flowering stem and the spicy seeds, which are strewn over savory pastries and bread and used to flavor casseroles, stews and soups.

CINNAMON & CASSIA

*C*INNAMON (Cinnamomum zeylanicum) *first came west from Sri Lanka as an Arab overland monopoly long before the Portuguese and the Dutch established their sea-borne empires. Sri Lanka and the Seychelles are still the main exporters of this most versatile spice, essential to Arab sweets and savories, Moghul garam masala, Mexican cinnamon tea and German apple strudel.*

Cinnamon

Cassia

The bark of the tree is taken from young shoots cut close to the ground once every two years in the rainy season. After the rough outer bark is planed off, these strips are dried, curling into characteristic quills. Essential oil is steam distilled from bits of bark. The fragrance of cinnamon is strongest when freshly ground.

CASSIA (*C. cassia*) does not have the outer bark removed, is thicker and coarser than cinnamon but also more pungent, better suited to pilafs and curries than sweet dishes. It is one of the Chinese Five Spices (p. 23).

CORIANDER

*C*ORIANDER (Coriandrum sativum) *spread through Europe with the Roman conquest but had earlier been known in China. India, the Middle East and Egypt. It was introduced into the New World in 1670 and was at that time extensively cultivated in England (East Anglia and Essex). It is now grown in all of the northern hemisphere, especially India.*

The sweet and aromatic taste of coriander, a bit like orange peel, is heightened by gentle roasting. In curry mixes and in the Moghul garam masalas, coriander usually provides the largest quantity of any spice. Europe has long had a rather different use for it—in stuffings and as a sausage spice. It is good with fish and with roast pork and lamb.

In Europe and America it is a traditional pickling spice, but it also has a widespread use in sweet dishes, breads and cakes.

Coriander

CUMIN

*C*UMIN (Cuminum cyminum), *probably a native of the Mediterranean but long cultivated in the warmer zones of Europe, India and China, is an unusual member of the aromatic umbellifers for being a low sprawling plant with fewer flowers and larger seeds than any of the others. It was popular in England until the 17th century but thereafter replaced by caraway.*

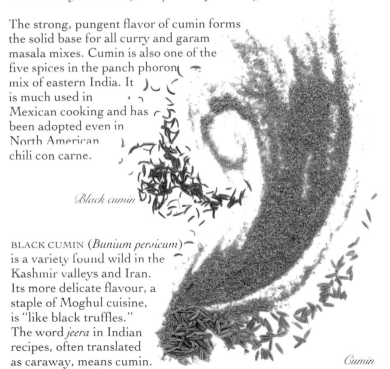

The strong, pungent flavor of cumin forms the solid base for all curry and garam masala mixes. Cumin is also one of the five spices in the panch phoron mix of eastern India. It is much used in Mexican cooking and has been adopted even in North American chili con carne.

Black cumin

BLACK CUMIN (*Bunium persicum*) is a variety found wild in the Kashmir valleys and Iran. Its more delicate flavour, a staple of Moghul cuisine, is "like black truffles." The word *jeera* in Indian recipes, often translated as caraway, means cumin.

Cumin

DILL & FENNEL

$\mathcal{F}$ENNEL (Foeniculum vulgare) *is a native of the Medi-terranean region and southern Europe, naturalized in temper-ate zones from India to South America. The plant is cultivated equally as a vegetable and as a source of seed. It is so closely related to dill that if the two are grown together they will freely cross-pollinate.*

Fennel, used whole or ground, has a flavor resembling anise but less sweet, more versatile. It is used in Italian salami and pasta sauce, in Indian vegetable dishes and Iraqi pastries. It is one of the five spices of Bengali panch phoron, and is equally at home in seafood dishes, candy or cordials.

Fennel

DILL (*Anethum graveolens*) is also a native of Europe but has been naturalized throughout North America. Popular in Scandinavian and Russian baking but also in casseroles and salads. In India a larger variety (*A. sowa*) is used. Taste and essential oil are much like those of caraway.

Dill

FENUGREEK

*F*ENUGREEK (Trigonella foenum-graecum), *native of west-ern Asia, has been cultivated in India (where the plant is eaten as a vegetable) and around the Mediterranean since prehistoric times. It is perhaps the only ancient herb cultivated in modern times for its medicinal properties: fenugreek is the main source of diosgenin, an important substance in the fabrication of oral contraceptives and sex hormones.*

As easy to grow in the home as are mustard or cress, it makes a good if unusual salad herb.

Fenugreek

Fenugreek is not really a spice but a very hard pulse. Its bitter-sweet, warm flavor, which comes out fully only when roasted and ground, is reminiscent of celery. It is essential to all curry mixes.

MUSTARD

*M*USTARDS *are members of the large*
Cruciferae *family, which includes all the*
cabbages. They are probably natives of the Mediterranean region
and southern Europe, where they have also been cultivated from very
early times for medicinal as well as culinary purposes.
In America mustard consumption is second only to that of pepper.
Mustards are now grown in most temperate climates,
often doubling as honey crops.

WHITE MUSTARD (*Brassica hirta*), the mustard of mustard and cress, has long grown wild in much of Europe and North America. It is a strong preservative used in pickles, and a good emulsifier in mayonnaise.

Its pale sandy-beige seeds have a pleasant nutty taste, but are not as pungent as the black variety. They are much used in American prepared mustards but forbidden in Dijon. Whole-grain mustards are usually made from a mix of both.

White mustard

Whole-grain mustard

Mustard powder

Smooth mustard

PREPARED MUSTARD has a flavor due to essential oil released only when mustard flour is mixed with water. English mustard, made up with fine flour and water shortly before use, is hotter than Continental and U.S. mustards made with a light vinegar and flavorings. Commercial mustard derives its color from turmeric.

BLACK MUSTARD (*Brassica nigra*) is being replaced by closely related INDIAN MUSTARD (*B. juncea*) because the latter is easier to produce. In Indian cooking brown (confusingly often called black) mustard is to the south what cumin is to the north, and mustard paste is a favorite flavor in Bengal.

Black Mustard

POPPY

*P*OPPY (Papaver somniferum), *a native of the Middle East, known in ancient Egypt and Persia to provide medicinal opium, which oozes out of cuts in unripe pods but is not present in the ripe seeds. Poppies bear white, pink or yellow flowers and also yield different coloured seed —blue-gray is common in Europe, creamy-yellow in India—which all have the same pleasant nutty flavor and crunchy texture.*

Brown poppy seed

India grinds the seeds to thicken stews, the Middle East makes them into sweets, Europe stops at decorative use on cakes or bread. In Turkey a brown strain called *haşhaş* (middle picture) is mixed with grape syrup and nuts for a dessert.

Yellow poppy seed

Blue-gray poppy seed

SESAME

*S*ESAME (Sesamum indicum), *probably of African origin, is now common also in tropical and subtropical Asia and the Mediterranean area. It is a food rather than a spice. Its oil, rich in polyunsaturated fats, is the main cooking oil of the Near and Far East — and a major ingredient of margarines. The residual cake is a protein-rich cattle fodder. Its slightly sweet and (after light toasting) nutty flavor has made sesame a popular condiment.*

Throughout Asia sesame is used in sweets; Chinese *niu bi tang* is perhaps the most widely known. In Europe and North America its use is mainly in the decoration of breads and cakes, but sesame cookies are widely available and sesame is fine in a sauce for fish.

Sesame seed

TAHINA, an emulsion from finely ground sesame seeds, is a staple flavoring in Middle Eastern dressings and dips such as the popular chick-pea-based humus. Halva, a favorite sweet of the region, is also made of sesame.

Tahina

UNUSUAL SPICES

THE VARIETY OF SPICES OBTAINABLE, *perhaps not always in the local supermarket, but with very little more trouble from* the shops that cater to specific ethnic groups, has become bewilderingly large. Some of these spices have never been familiar in European or North American kitchens but are absolutely basic to the cuisine of other parts of the world. Sumac, for instance, is to the Arab world what tamarind is to much of Asia or lemon juice to the West—always on hand, a necessity. With the exception of fresh curry leaves and lemon grass, the spices shown here will keep for several months.

LEMON OR CITRONELLA GRASS (*Cymbopogon citratus*) is a common grass of Southeast Asia with the strong smell and taste of lemon. It is widely cultivated for its oil. Lemongrass is used fresh, dried, whole or powdered, in fish dishes, soups and sauces.

Safflower

Lemon-grass

SAFFLOWER (*Carthamus tinctorius*) has a dye that can give food a saffron color but not its taste. It is used as decorative garnish in many Turkish dishes.

SUMAC (*Rhus coriora*) is used as a souring agent in Arab cooking, to flavor kebabs and fish dishes. American Indians used red sumac, a common shrub, for a sour drink.

Sumac

Nigella

NIGELLA (*Nigella sativa*) is used in India for vegetable dishes, and sprinkled over bread. In the Middle East it is used in candy making. Its flavor is not unlike cumin.

AJOWAN or carom (*Carum copticum*) is used in India, Egypt and Iran in rich pastries and bean dishes, both for its powerful thymelike taste and to control flatulence.

Ajowan

CURRY LEAVES (from *Murraya koenigii*, a hardwood tree which grows in the Himalayan foothills and in many South Asian gardens) impart a "curry" flavor to vegetarian dishes. They are used whole, often on the stem for ease of removal. Fresh leaves keep in a refrigerator and are much better than dried.

Curry leaves

ORIENTAL SPICE MIXES

*W*HERE WESTERN COOKING *on the whole prefers to give a dish a specific flavor based on one or at most a few spices, Asia has developed an enormous range of spice mixes with a very complex character. The true merit of a blend lies in the way each ingredient is allowed to make its own specific contribution to a dish without interfering with any of the other components. In India a good chef will have been a good* masalchi *(blender of spices)* first.

GARAM MASALA is the general name for a family of spice mixes which can be hot (chili, cloves) or aromatic (mace, cinnamon, cardamom) but which should always be used sparingly.

KASHMIR MASALA, from the great northernmost valley of India. It is a crumbly paste with a coriander base to which chilies and ginger give a pungent glow.

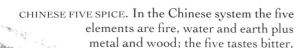

CHINESE FIVE SPICE. In the Chinese system the five elements are fire, water and earth plus metal and wood; the five tastes bitter, sweet, sour, salty and pungent; and the five spices usually Sichuan pepper, fennel, clove, cassia and star anise. This mixture is finely ground and used mostly in marinades for poultry, meat or fish.

VINDALOO PASTE is one of the few really hot Indian spice mixes. It comes from Goa, where many of the condiments are rather fiery. It is based on chili peppers, tempered with cinnamon and coriander, cumin turmeric, garlic and ginger, and mixed to a paste with vinegar.

Recipes

*All recipes will serve 4,
but some (such as pastries and breads)
will serve more.*

THAI PRAWN SOUP

6 cups/1.5 liters fish or chicken
stock
3 stalks lemongrass, sliced and
pounded
2 green chilies, seeded and sliced
peel of 1 lime
1 lb/500 g large prawns, shelled
juice of 2 limes
4 scallions, sliced
3 tablespoons coarsely chopped
coriander leaves
1 small red chili, seeded and sliced

Put the stock, lemongrass,
green chilies and lime peel into
a pan and bring to the boil.
Cover and simmer for 20
minutes, then strain. Return the
stock to the pan, add the prawns
and simmer for 3-4 minutes.
Stir in the lime juice and remove
from the heat. Garnish with
scallions, coriander and red
chili and serve at once.

SOLE IN SOUR CREAM

4 fillets of sole or turbot
salt and pepper
1/2 teaspoon ground anise or
fennel seeds
1 oz/25 g butter
2/3 cup/150 ml sour cream

Sprinkle the fish with salt,
pepper and anise or fennel
and put it into a lightly buttered
oven dish. Spread the sour
cream over the fish and dot with
the remaining butter. Cover the
dish and bake in a preheated
oven, 350°F, 180°C for
25-30 minutes.

MARINATED HERRING

4 herrings, filleted
1/2 cup/125 ml milk
1 tablespoon prepared mustard
1 1/4 cups/300 ml vinegar
1 bouquet garni
1 small onion, chopped
4 peppercorns
4 whole allspice
a few dill seeds
1/4 cup/50 ml oil
1 teaspoon salt

Soak the herrings for 3 hours in
salted milk. Drain and pat dry,
then spread the flesh with
mustard and roll up with the
skin on the outside. Secure each
roll with a toothpick and put
them in a large jar. Bring the
vinegar to the boil with the
bouquet garni, onion and spices
and cook for 10 minutes. Cool
slightly, remove the bouquet
garni and stir in the oil.

Pour the marinade over the
herrings, close the jar
and keep for 2-3 days in
the refrigerator
before serving.

CURRIED FISH STEAKS

4 fish steaks
1 teaspoon mustard seeds
2 dried chilies
1 small ball tamarind[1] or
juice of 1 lemon
3 tablespoons oil
2 onions, chopped
2 cloves garlic, chopped
2 tablespoons curry powder
small piece fresh ginger, chopped
3 curry leaves
salt

Grind the mustard seeds and chilies. Soak the tamarind in 4 tablespoons warm water until soft, then squeeze and crumble it. Strain out any fibrous bits. Heat the oil and fry the onion and garlic until golden. Stir in the ground spices and fry for another minute or two Add the ginger, curry leaves and tamarind water and a little salt. Put in the fish, cover and simmer for 8-10 minutes or until the fish is cooked and the sauce quite thick.

1. Tamarind is a pleasantly sharp pulp extracted from the pods of a tropical tree. It is most conveniently bought in small balls coated with sugar.

LAMB KORMA

1½ lb/750 g lean lamb, cubed
1¼ cups/300 ml yogurt
2 onions, chopped
2 in/5 cm fresh ginger, chopped
2 tablespoons garam masala
½ teaspoon salt
⅔ cup/150 ml heavy cream
¼ cup/50 g cashew nuts
¼ cup/50 g raisins

Put the yogurt, onions and ginger in a blender and purée.

Put the purée, garam masala, salt, cream and lamb into a heavy pan, bring gently to the boil, then cover tightly and simmer on the lowest possible heat for 1½ hours. Stir frequently during cooking to make sure it is not sticking to the bottom of the pan. Stir in the nuts and raisins and cook for another 10 minutes, then serve with rice.

KEBAB FROM THE CAUCASUS

1½ lb/750 g lean lamb, cubed
1 onion
1 clove garlic
½ teaspoon black peppercorns
1 teaspoon coriander seeds
¼ teaspoon dill seeds
salt
juice of 1 lemon or 1 pomegranate
4–5 scallions
1 lemon
ground sumac
oil

Grate the onion, reserving the juice. Crush the garlic and spices lightly. Mix together the onion, garlic, spices, salt and lemon or pomegranate juice and marinate the lamb for at least 6 and up to 24 hours. Thread the meat onto skewers and grill for 8-10 minutes. If necessary brush the kebabs with a little oil from time to time. Garnish with chopped scallions, the lemon cut in wedges and serve with a bowl of sumac.

CHINESE BRAISED DUCK

4 lb/2 kg duck, quartered
1 tablespoon oil
1 leek, sliced thinly
1 clove garlic, chopped
small piece of fresh ginger, chopped
3 tablespoons sherry
5 tablespoons soy sauce
1 teaspoon brown sugar
good pinch salt
2 cups/450 ml hot stock
1 star anise
small piece of cassia or cinnamon
1 teaspoon Chinese Five Spice powder
2 teaspoons cornstarch
2 tablespoons water

Heat the oil in a heavy pan and brown the duck on all sides. Lift out the duck and fry the leek, garlic and ginger for 2 minutes. Mix together the sherry, soy sauce, sugar and salt. Put back the duck, and pour over the sherry mixture. Stir well, add the hot stock and spices. Cover the pan, lower the heat and braise for 50 minutes, or until the duck is tender. Transfer the duck to a heated serving dish. Blend the cornstarch into the water and pour the mixture into the pan. Stir until the sauce thickens and becomes clear, about 2–3 minutes. Pour it over the duck and serve.

AFELIA

1½ lb/750 g pork tenderloin
2 oz/50 g butter
salt and pepper
glass of red wine
4 teaspoons crushed coriander seeds

Remove any fat from the pork and cut into cubes. Melt the butter and brown the meat on all sides. Season with salt and pepper, add the wine, bring to the boil, then cover and simmer for 20 minutes. Stir in the coriander, replace the lid and simmer for another 20–25 minutes, until the meat is tender and most of the liquid absorbed. Serve with rice or a pilaf of cracked wheat.

GEORGIAN CHICKEN

1 small chicken cut in serving pieces
salt and pepper
1½ oz/40 g butter
2 large onions, chopped
1 lb/500 g tomatoes, peeled, seeded and chopped
6 tablespoons white wine
1 teaspoon coriander seeds, crushed
¼ teaspoon fenugreek
large pinch celery seeds
1 teaspoon safflower, crushed
1 bay leaf
½ teaspoon dried thyme
1 lemon, sliced thinly
4 tablespoons finely chopped dill

Season the chicken with salt and pepper and sauté the pieces in the butter in a heavy pan. When browned on all sides, remove them and cook the onions until golden brown. Add the tomatoes, wine, spices, bay leaf and thyme. Put back the chicken, lay the lemon slices on top, cover and simmer for 45–50 minutes, or until the chicken is tender. If the pan is getting too dry, add a little more wine or water. Sprinkle with dill before serving.

MALAY NOODLES

4 large dried red chilies
piece of fresh ginger, peeled and chopped
1 small onion, chopped
2 teaspoons ground coriander
¾ teaspoon ground anise
¾ teaspoon ground cumin
¼ teaspoon ground turmeric
3 tablespoons mustard or groundnut oil
2 cups/450 ml chicken stock
½ lb/250 g potatoes, boiled and mashed
¾ lb/375 g egg noodles
6 oz/175 g bean sprouts
handful of dry roasted peanuts

Remove the seeds and stalks from the chilies, chop them and grind or pound in a mortar with the ginger and onion. Add the ground spices and blend together.

Start boiling water in a large pan for the noodles. Heat the oil in a wok or heavy pan until it smokes and fry the spice mixture. Pour in the chicken stock, stir and simmer for 5 minutes. Stir in the mashed potato, a little at a time, until you have a smooth, thick sauce. Boil the noodles al dente, drain and put them into a serving dish. Pour over the sauce and garnish with the bean sprouts and peanuts.

ONION SALAD WITH SUMAC

Thinly slice *2 onions* and sprinkle with *¼ teaspoon ground sumac* and a little *salt*. Let stand for 30 minutes before serving. This salad is particularly good with kebabs and other grilled meats.

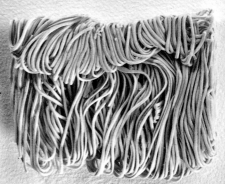

STUFFED MUSHROOMS

4 large flat mushrooms
2 tablespoons sesame seeds
2 oz/50 g butter
2 cloves garlic, crushed
handful of chopped parsley
1¼ cups/75 g fresh bread crumbs
pinch cayenne
3 tablespoons grated Parmesan

Toast the sesame seeds for a few minutes in a dry frying pan. Remove the stalks from the mushrooms and chop them.

Heat 2 oz/50 g butter in a frying pan and cook the tops of the mushrooms briefly. Remove them to a buttered ovenproof tray and cook the mushroom stalks and garlic for a few minutes. Stir in the other ingredients and remove the pan from the heat. Spread the mixture onto the mushrooms, dot with a little more butter and grill for 4–5 minutes.

INDIAN BRAISED POTATO AND EGGPLANT

1 lb/500 g potatoes
1 lb/500 g eggplant
2 onions
4 tablespoons oil
¾ teaspoon fennel seeds
½ teaspoon fenugreek seeds
2 teaspoons garam masala
¼ teaspoon cayenne
1 teaspoon mango powder or lemon juice
1 teaspoon salt

Cut the pototoes and eggplant into cubes and chop the onions coarsely. Heat the oil in a heavy pan, and when it is hot put in the fennel and fenugreek seeds and fry for a few seconds until they turn darker. Add the vegetables, lower the heat and fry, stirring and shaking the pan, for 10 minutes. Stir in the garam masala, cayenne, mango powder and salt. Add ¼ pint/150 ml water, cover the pan, lower the heat further and simmer for 15–20 minutes, turning the vegetables occasionally. Serve hot or at room temperature.

MOROCCAN ORANGE SALAD

Peel *4 large seedless oranges*,
remove all pith, and divide into segments. Arrange these
in a bowl, spoon over *2 tablespoons of orange
flower-water*, sprinkle with *cinnamon*.

CELERY SEED DRESSING

A good dressing for a winter
vegetable salad.

½ teaspoon celery seed
½ teaspoon dry mustard
pinch cayenne
3 tablespoons wine vinegar
⅔ cup/150 ml safflower oil
salt

Mix together the spices and
whisk in the vinegar and oil.
Taste and add salt if you wish.
Whisk until the dressing
thickens a little before using.

MANGO CHUTNEY

2 lb/1 kg green mango
2 cloves garlic
2 oz/50 g fresh ginger
½ teaspoon ground cinnamon
1 teaspoon chilli powder
½ teaspoon ground mace
½ teaspoon ground cumin
¾ cup/175 ml vinegar
12 green cardamoms
2 lb/1 kg sugar
1 teaspoon salt
2 oz/50 g blanched almonds, flaked
4 oz/125 g raisins

Peel and grate the mangoes.
Crush the garlic, peel and chop
the ginger and combine with the
ground spices and a little of the
vinegar to make a smooth paste.
Discard the skins of the
cardamoms. Put the mangoes
and sugar in a large heavy pan
and cook over medium heat for
10 minutes, then stir in the spice
paste and cardamom seeds and
cook slowly until the mixture
has the consistency of a jam,
about 40 minutes. Add the
remaining vinegar and salt and
cook for another 10 minutes or
so until it becomes a thick
purée. Stir in the almonds and
raisins, leave to cool and then
pot.

POTATO AND POMEGRANATE SALAD

1 lb/500 g potatoes
½ cucumber
1 small pomegranate
1 small mild onion
3 tablespoons lemon juice
4 tablespoons oil
1 teaspoon chat masala (p. 37)
1 teaspoon ground cumin
mint leaves

Boil the potatoes and cut into cubes. Remove the seeds from the cucumber and cube it. Take the pomegranate seeds from the fruit, discarding all the pith. Slice the onion finely. Mix the lemon juice, oil, chat masala and cumin to make a dressing. Put the potatoes, cucumber and most of the pomegranate and onion into a bowl and toss with the dressing. Garnish with the remaining pomegranate seeds and onion rings and the mint leaves.

CUMIN VINAIGRETTE

½ teaspoon ground cumin
2 tablespoons wine vinegar
6 tablespoons olive oil
2 teaspoons honey
salt and pepper

Whisk all the ingredients together and use to dress carrot salad or a salad of bitter greens such as chicory, endive or radicchio.

OLIVES WITH CORIANDER

1 lb/500 g whole green olives in brine
4–5 cloves garlic
1 tablespoon coriander seeds, crushed
lightly
½ lemon, sliced
1 bay leaf
olive oil

Drain and rinse the olives. Crack them by hitting with a rolling pin or mallet and put them into a large jar interspersed with the garlic, coriander, lemon and bay leaf. Cover with olive oil. Keep the jar in a cool place for 2–3 weeks before using.

Variation

Use fennel seeds instead of coriander.

DILL PICKLES

2 lb/1 kg small pickling cucumbers
a few dill or fennel stalks (optional)
1¼ cups/300 ml white vinegar
2½ cups/600 ml water
2 tablespoons dill seeds
1 tablespoon white peppercorns
½ cup/50 g coarse salt

Use fresh firm cucumbers and put them in the coldest part of the refrigerator for 24 hours before pickling—this helps keep them crisp. Put the cucumbers, cut in half lengthways if you wish, into large preserving jars with the dill or fennel stalks among them. Bring the vinegar, water, spices and salt to the boil and pour, boiling hot, over the cucumbers. Make sure they are completely immersed. Let them cool, then cover. Store for 2–3 weeks before eating.

ARAB BREAD WITH SPICES

½ packet quick-rising yeast or
¼ oz/7 g dried yeast
1 lb/500 g bread flour
1 teaspoon salt
about 2 cups/450 ml warm water
olive oil
¾ cup/75 g zahtar (p. 37)

If using quick-rising yeast sprinkle it over the flour with the salt. Put ordinary dried yeast to prove in a little warm water and then stir into the flour. Add enough water to mix to a fairly stiff dough. Turn onto a floured surface and knead until smooth and elastic. Clean the mixing bowl, oil lightly and put in the ball of dough, turning to coat with oil on all sides. Cover with plastic wrap or a cloth and let it double in bulk—about 1½ hours.

Punch down and divide in two, or into small pieces to make individual breads. Form the two loaves into circles about 5 in/12 cm in diameter or the small pieces into circles 3 in/7 cm in diameter and ¼ in/5 mm thick.

Put the bread on a greased baking sheet, cover and let rise again for 30 minutes. Spread the tops with a paste of olive oil and zahtar and bake in a preheated oven 400°F, 200°C for 10–12 minutes. The small breads will be ready then, so take them out and stack to keep them soft.

For the larger loaves, lower the oven to 350°F, 160°C and bake for a further 20–25 minutes. The loaves should sound hollow when tapped on the bottom.

Variations

Brush the tops of the breads with beaten egg and sprinkle thickly with nigella, poppy or sesame seeds. Instead of putting spices on the bread, the Moroccans add 1½ teaspoons each of anise and sesame to the dough.

GARAM MASALA

2 tablespoons green cardamoms
2 long sticks cinnamon
2 tablespoons black peppercorns
3 tablespoons cumin seeds
3 tablespoons coriander seeds
1/2 nutmeg
1 tablespoon cloves

Remove the cardamom seeds from the pods. Combine all the spices and roast in a medium oven or a dry pan until darkened in color—about 8 minutes. Let them cool, then grind and store in an airtight container.

CARAWAY AND SALT STRAWS

4 oz/125 g butter
2 1/4 cups/250 g flour
4 tablespoons sour cream
1 egg yolk
caraway seeds
coarse salt

Rub the butter into the flour until the texture is crumbly, then bind with the cream to make a dough. Form into a ball and chill for 30 minutes. Roll out the dough on a floured surface and cut into sticks. Brush with beaten egg yolk and sprinkle with caraway seeds and salt. Bake in a preheated oven, 400°F, 200°C for 10–12 minutes.

"CURRIE POWDER

cayenne pepper 3 oz   cummin seed 6 oz
ginger powder'd 6 oz   fenugreek seed 3 oz
coriander seed 10 oz   black pepper 2 oz
cardamom seed 6 oz   best pale turmeric 10 oz"

From a manuscript recipe book, 1865

CHAT MASALA

1 tablespoon cumin
1 tablespoon black pepper
½ teaspoon ajowan
2 teaspoons coarse salt
¼ teaspoon ground asafoetida
1 teaspoon mango powder
1 teaspoon ground ginger
½ teaspoon cayenne

Grind the first three spices and the salt to a powder. Stir in the remaining ingredients and mix well. Store in an airtight container.

ZAHTAR

This is a highly aromatic mixture from the Middle East which is sprinkled on meatballs or vegetables or used as a dip. Mixed to a thick paste with olive oil it makes an excellent topping for Arab bread (p. 35). The proportions can be varied to suit your own taste.

½ cup/50 g sesame seeds
2 tablespoons ground sumac
2 tablespoons ground dried thyme

Toast the sesame seeds in the oven for a few minutes then mix with the sumac and thyme. Store in an airtight container.

WALNUT PASTRIES

2¼ cups/250 g flour
½ teaspoon ground fennel seeds
(optional)
¼ teaspoon nigella (optional)
3 teaspoons superfine sugar
pinch of salt
4 oz/125 g butter
2–3 tablespoons water
1¼ cups/175 g walnuts, chopped
seeds of 2 cardamoms, crushed or
¼ teaspoon ground cinnamon
2 tablespoons honey
grated rind of ½ lemon
1 egg
confectioners' sugar

Put the flour, fennel and nigella, 1 teaspoon sugar and the salt into a bowl and rub in the butter until the mixture resembles bread crumbs. Add enough water to mix to a soft dough. Form into a ball and chill for 30 minutes.

Prepare the filling by mixing together the walnuts, 2 teaspoons sugar, the spice, honey and lemon rind.

Roll out the pastry on a floured surface and cut into 4 in/10 cm circles. Put a spoonful of filling on each circle and fold over to make a half moon. Seal the edges well. Prick each one with a fork and brush with beaten egg. Transfer the pastries to a cookie sheet and bake in a preheated oven 375°F, 190°C for 15–20 minutes. Do not overbake. Let them cool, then sprinkle with confectioners' sugar.

SEED CAKE

"4 oz/125 g butter
⅔ cup/125 g sugar
2 eggs
1 cup/125 g flour
1 teaspoon caraway seeds
pinch of salt

Cream butter and sugar, whisk yolks and whites of eggs separately, add, gradually, flour, yolks and whites, also caraway seeds. Bake half-hour to three-quarters hour in quick oven."
Cornish Recipes, 1929,
The Cornwall Federation of Women's Institutes

Poppy Seed and Honey Ice Cream

1 1/4 cups/300 ml milk
1 vanilla bean
3 egg yolks
1/4 cup/50 g sugar
1/2 cup/125 g honey
2/3 cup/75 g poppy seeds
2/3 cup/150 ml whipping cream

Heat the milk with the vanilla bean and bring to boil. Remove from the heat and leave to infuse for 10 minutes. Meanwhile whisk the egg yolks and sugar together until thick and pale. Put the bowl over a pan of simmering water. Remove the vanilla bean and whisk the milk into the egg mixture. Stir constantly until it thickens enough to coat the back of a spoon. Do not let it boil.

Remove from the heat and stir in the honey and the poppy seeds. Let cool. Whip the cream to soft peaks and fold into the custard. Freeze in an ice cream machine.

Poppy Seed Pastries

2/3 cup/75 g poppy seeds, ground
1/3 cup/50 g toasted almonds, ground
2 teaspoons sugar
3 tablespoons honey
pastry as in Walnut Pastries (p. 38)

Mix together the poppy seeds, almonds and sugar, then add the honey to form a thick paste. Use instead of the walnut filling in the Walnut Pastries recipe.

INDEX

ACKNOWLEDGMENTS

The publishers
would like to thank the
following people:

· ILLUSTRATOR ·
JANE THOMSON

JACKET
· PHOTOGRAPHY ·
DAVE KING

DESIGN
· ASSISTANCE ·
SUE CORNER

· TYPESETTING ·
WYVERN
TYPESETTING LTD

· REPRODUCTION ·
COLOURSCAN
SINGAPORE

PAGE 5. MARY EVANS PICTURE LIBRARY